The Best Ever

BREAD BOOK

LIZZIE MUNSEY

CONSULTANT EMILY MUNSEY

The first Munsey millers, in 1911

Emily and Lizzie Munsey

Stacks of flour in the mill

Introduction

Our family has been milling flour in Oxfordshire, England, since 1895. When we were little, the mill was looked after by our grandfather, Bill, and our dad, Paul. Now Emily runs it with Paul.

We have spent our whole lives surrounded by milling, flour, and grain. If it was Dad's turn to pick us up from school, he would sometimes show up in a flour truck. We baked together after school and fed grain to the ducks that lived on the mill stream.

This book will take you on a milling journey all the way from the wheat in a farmer's field to freshly made bread in a bakery.

We hope you enjoy it!

Lizzie Munsey

Emily Munsey

Emily Munsey, Flour Miller

Wessex Mill in Oxfordshire, UK

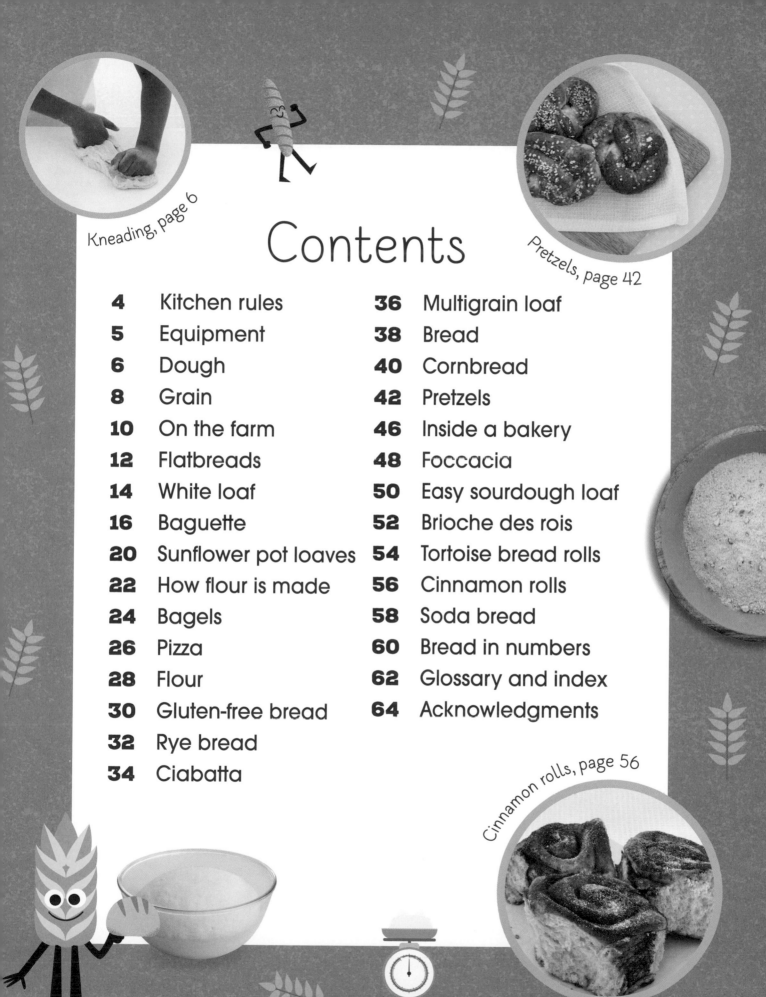

Kneading, page 6

Pretzels, page 42

Contents

Cinnamon rolls, page 56

Kitchen rules

Baking is fun! Here is what you'll need to know before you get started. You will need an adult to help you with all the recipes in this book.

KITCHEN SAFETY

Be very careful...

• When you see the warning triangle, take extra care and ask an adult for help.

• Be careful around hot ovens and gas or electric burners, making sure you know whether the oven or stovetop is on, and protecting your hands when **touching or lifting anything hot** from, or on, or into it. **Oven mitts** are your friends here!

• Take extra care when handling hot liquids or hot pans, watching carefully for spills and protecting your hands (using oven mitts or a dish towel) when moving or holding hot items. Tell an adult immediately if you get a burn.

• Be careful when handling anything sharp, such as knives or a grater. Take extra care when cutting dough with a sharp knife.

• When using power tools such as food processors and mixers, check if they're on and don't put your hands near the moving parts until you have switched them off at the socket.

WHEN IN DOUBT, ask an ADULT to help, especially when you're unsure about anything.

INGREDIENTS AND EQUIPMENT

• Make sure you have all your ingredients laid out before you start to make a recipe. You'll probably have most ingredients in your kitchen already, but some you will need to buy.

• Always use the type of flour specified in a recipe—bread, all-purpose, or self-rising.

• Use medium-sized, free-range eggs, unless stated otherwise.

• For recipes that require milk, you can use whole milk, low-fat, or skim.

Preheating the oven

Follow the temperature instructions within each recipe.

Special equipment

Keep an eye out for recipes that require special equipment. Buy or borrow items in advance if you don't own them.

KITCHEN HYGIENE

Please note that when you're in the kitchen, you need to follow these important rules to keep germs in check.

• Always wash your hands before you start any recipe.

• Use hot, soapy water to clean cutting boards after each use.

• Keep your cooking area clean and have a cloth handy to mop up any spills.

• Always check the use-by date on all ingredients.

• Wash your hands after handling raw eggs.

WEIGHTS AND MEASUREMENTS

Carefully weigh the ingredients before you start a recipe. Use measuring spoons, weighing scales, and a measuring cup, as necessary. Below are the abbreviations and full names for the measurements used in this book.

Metric	US measures	Spoon measures
g = gram	oz = ounce	tsp = teaspoon
kg = kilogram	lb = pound	tbsp = tablespoon
ml = milliliter	fl oz = fluid ounce	
cm = centimeter	in = inch	

Equipment

Here is the kitchen equipment that is used in this book. You won't need to use everything shown here for every recipe!

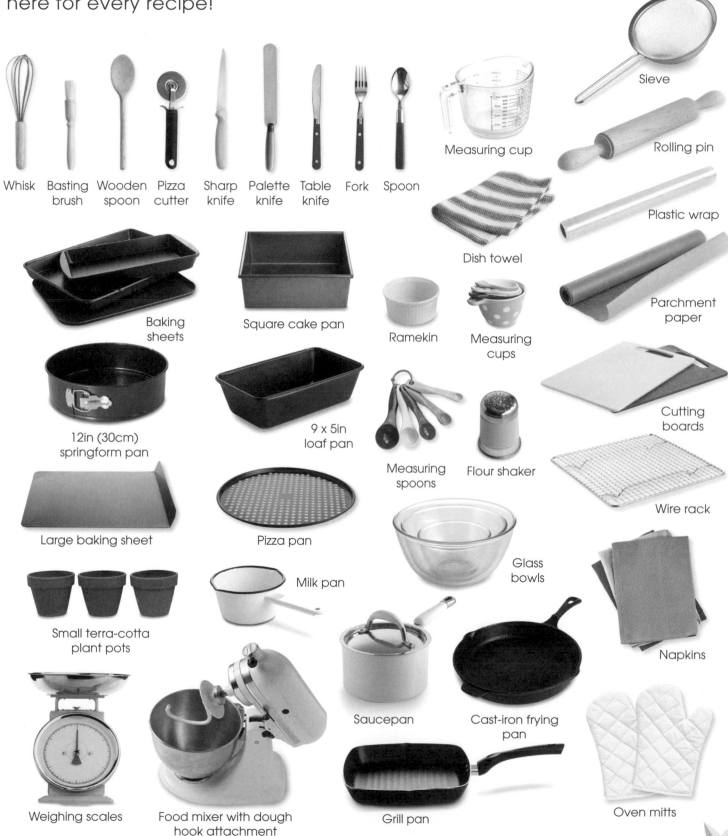

Whisk

Basting brush

Wooden spoon

Pizza cutter

Sharp knife

Palette knife

Table knife

Fork

Spoon

Measuring cup

Sieve

Rolling pin

Plastic wrap

Dish towel

Parchment paper

Baking sheets

Square cake pan

Ramekin

Measuring cups

12in (30cm) springform pan

9 x 5in loaf pan

Measuring spoons

Flour shaker

Cutting boards

Wire rack

Large baking sheet

Pizza pan

Glass bowls

Milk pan

Small terra-cotta plant pots

Saucepan

Cast-iron frying pan

Napkins

Weighing scales

Food mixer with dough hook attachment

Grill pan

Oven mitts

5

Dough

All bread begins as a mixture of flour and water called dough. The steps we follow to make dough are similar for most types of bread.

Use a spoon at first, then your hands, if that's easier.

Kneading

When we make dough, we push and pull it around in a process called **kneading**. Working the dough like this warms and stretches out a substance called **gluten**.

1 Bring the ingredients together and keep mixing until there is no flour left on the sides of the bowl.

You can use a scraper to help bring your dough back into a ball and keep your surface clean.

↑ **Dough scraper**

2 The dough will become smooth and less sticky. Once it is a single lump, place it on a lightly floured surface.

3 Use one hand to hold your dough down at the back. Then put the heel of your hand in the middle of your dough.

4 Push your front hand away from you, stretching the dough forward and away from you.

What makes bread rise?

Some bread is flat. But many breads are made using something called a rising agent, which adds air to the dough, making the finished bread light and fluffy. The most common rising agent is yeast.

Sugars

Yeast eating the sugars

Gas

Unactivated yeast

← Yeast

How it works

Yeast is alive! It is a type of fungus, similar to mushrooms. It has egg-shaped cells that are so tiny we cannot see them without a microscope.

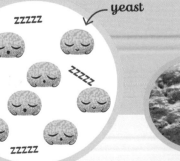

When yeast is added to a dough, it eats sugars in the flour and produces bubbles of gas.

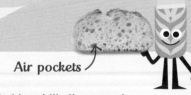

Air pockets ↙

Baking kills the yeast, but the gas bubbles are trapped in the bread, creating tiny pockets of air throughout the loaf.

5 Fold the stretched part of the dough back onto itself. Gently push the ends together.

6 Turn your dough around 90 degrees (a quarter turn) before you stretch it out again.

7 Keep going! Repeat these steps over and over again, until the dough is smooth and springy.

8 Once the dough is ready, it should be smooth and spring back if you poke a finger into it.

How kneading works

There are two types of protein in flour: gliadin and glutenin. As the dough is kneaded, the strands of these proteins are stretched out and mixed together, forming gluten.

Gliadin

Glutenin

Gluten

Gluten is strong and elastic. It can capture the bubbles of air made by the yeast.

Power kneading

Kneading doesn't have to be done by hand. Many home bakers now use an electric mixer with a "dough hook" to knead their bread for them.

Proofing

Yeast doesn't work instantly. After yeast has been added to the dough, the dough is left for an hour or so, so the yeast can get to work. This is called proofing.

Salt is added to dough to slow down the action of the yeast, so the bread doesn't rise too quickly.

Before
Before the dough is proofed, it is dense and heavy, with no air bubbles in it.

During
The dough steadily fills with air as the yeast gets to work.

After
Once the dough has proofed, it is almost twice its original size. We say that it has "risen."

Rising agents

Here are some rising agents that are used in baking:

Baking powder

This is often used for baking cakes, although it can be used to make quick bread recipes such as soda bread.

Yeast

There are two main types of yeast—fresh and dry. Fresh yeast comes as a paste. It has to be kept in the fridge and used up quickly. Dry yeast comes as a powder and lasts much longer.

Sourdough starter

A sourdough starter is living yeast. It must be kept in the fridge and regularly "fed" with flour and water to keep it alive.

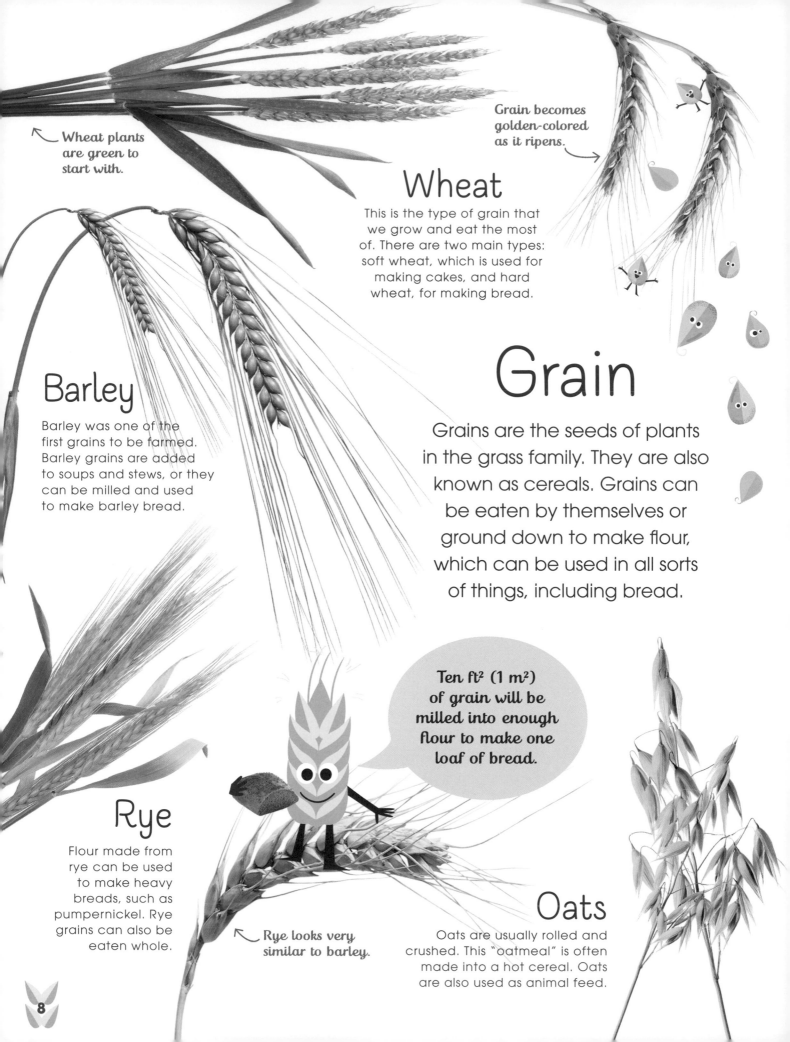

Wheat plants are green to start with.

Grain becomes golden-colored as it ripens.

Wheat

This is the type of grain that we grow and eat the most of. There are two main types: soft wheat, which is used for making cakes, and hard wheat, for making bread.

Barley

Barley was one of the first grains to be farmed. Barley grains are added to soups and stews, or they can be milled and used to make barley bread.

Grain

Grains are the seeds of plants in the grass family. They are also known as cereals. Grains can be eaten by themselves or ground down to make flour, which can be used in all sorts of things, including bread.

Ten ft² (1 m²) of grain will be milled into enough flour to make one loaf of bread.

Rye

Flour made from rye can be used to make heavy breads, such as pumpernickel. Rye grains can also be eaten whole.

Rye looks very similar to barley.

Oats

Oats are usually rolled and crushed. This "oatmeal" is often made into a hot cereal. Oats are also used as animal feed.

Millet

There are many different types of millet. They are grown in dry places all over the world. Millet is usually used to make flat breads or porridge.

Millet has very small seeds.

Spelt is closely related to wheat.

Spelt

This is an ancient grain that has been farmed since around 5,000 BCE. It can be used whole or ground into flour. Spelt bread has an unusual nutty flavor.

Off the stalk

When grains are taken off the stalk, they look very different—like a pile of little ovals. Grains must be taken off their stalks before they can be milled.

Wheat grains

Buckwheat

Buckwheat is usually ground down to make flour. The flour is used to make noodles, pancakes, and porridge.

Einkorn

This grain is believed to be the first wheat ever farmed. It was first grown around 10,000 years ago in what is now Turkey.

Sorghum

Sorghum grows well in dry places. There are many varieties, in a rainbow of colors, including white, yellow, red, and purple. The grains are eaten by people and fed to animals.

Buckwheat grains have hard outer shells.

On the farm

Wheat doesn't grow by itself. Planting and tending to wheat is a full-time job for millions of farmers around the world.

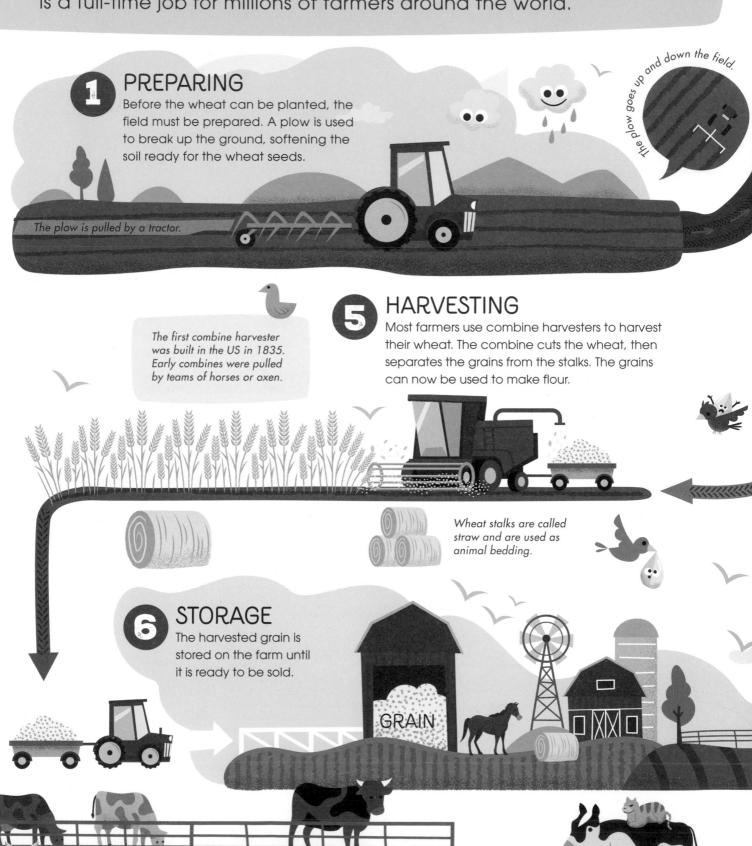

1 PREPARING

Before the wheat can be planted, the field must be prepared. A plow is used to break up the ground, softening the soil ready for the wheat seeds.

The plow goes up and down the field.

The plow is pulled by a tractor.

5 HARVESTING

Most farmers use combine harvesters to harvest their wheat. The combine cuts the wheat, then separates the grains from the stalks. The grains can now be used to make flour.

The first combine harvester was built in the US in 1835. Early combines were pulled by teams of horses or oxen.

Wheat stalks are called straw and are used as animal bedding.

6 STORAGE

The harvested grain is stored on the farm until it is ready to be sold.

GRAIN

② PLANTING

Wheat seeds are planted by a grain drill, which is pulled behind a tractor. It makes a shallow trench in the soil, which it drops the seeds into, then covers them evenly with soil.

Grain drill

③ FERTILIZING

To help the wheat grow, fertilizer is sprayed onto it. This liquid contains nitrogen, which the wheat needs to grow, helping it become strong, with lots of seeds (grains).

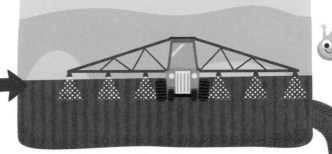

The seeds must be planted at exactly the right depth.

If the seeds aren't covered, birds will eat them.

If they are buried too deeply, the seedlings won't be able to grow.

If there is not enough rain, the crop will not grow well, and the farmer will not be able to harvest much wheat.

④ RIPE WHEAT

The wheat is ready to harvest when it turns golden and there is no green visible on the plant.

I'm ripe and ready to harvest!

Leaves

Wheat is ready to harvest when all the plants in the field have become golden.

Ripe   Flowering   Growing   Sprouting

⑦ TO THE MILL!

Special trucks collect the wheat to take it to the mill. Only the best quality wheat will be used for flour.

Wheat grains

Growing crops such as wheat is called "arable" farming.

Flatbreads

People have eaten flatbreads for thousands of years, and most parts of the world have their own type. Some flatbreads have nothing in them to make the bread rise, but these recipes use yeast and baking powder.

The oldest known flatbread was discovered in Jordan. It is more than 14,400 years old!

10 mins

1 hr rising, 9–16 mins cooking

6 flatbreads

Ingredients:

- 1½ cups + 1 tbsp bread flour, plus extra for dusting
- 1 tsp instant dry yeast
- ½ tsp granulated sugar
- ½ tsp salt
- ¾ cup lukewarm water

Pita bread

Naan

To make naan bread, use the flatbread recipe, but in step 1 leave out the sugar and water. Instead, add an egg and 3 tablespoons of plain yogurt. Follow these instructions when you get to step 5, kneading the dough first.

Naan bread

5 Roll each chunk into a teardrop shape. Sprinkle a teaspoon of cumin seeds over each naan. Preheat a baking sheet under a broiler.

6 Carefully place the naans on the hot baking sheet and glaze both sides with melted butter. Broil for 2–3 minutes on each side.

1 Place the flour, yeast, sugar, and salt in a large mixing bowl. Mix with a wooden spoon. Make a well in the center and stir in enough of the water to form a soft dough.

2 Place the dough on a lightly floured surface and knead for 5 minutes, until it is smooth and elastic.

3 Return the dough to the bowl and cover with a clean, damp dish towel. Leave it in a warm place for 1 hour, or until the dough has doubled in size.

4 Punch down into the dough with your fist to remove the large air bubbles. Then divide the dough into 6 equal chunks.

5 Knead each chunk gently on a lightly floured surface. Roll each piece of dough out into a circle around 5in (13cm) across. Preheat a frying pan.

6 Carefully fry each flatbread for 1 minute. Then flip each one over and cook the other side for 30 seconds. Serve immediately.

Tortilla

Use the flatbread recipe, but in step 1 leave out the yeast and sugar. Instead, add ½ tsp of baking powder and ¼ cup of lard or, vegetable shortening. Skip step 3. At step 4, knead the dough and divide into 8 chunks. Then follow these steps.

5 Roll each chunk into a thin circle shape. Layer them in a pile with wax paper between each tortilla. Preheat pan to a medium-high heat.

6 Carefully fry each tortilla in the pan for 1 minute. Then turn the tortilla over and fry the other side for 1 minute.

Tortillas

White loaf

A classic white loaf can be made with only a little effort and a few simple ingredients. The finished loaf is perfect for making toast or sandwiches.

The yeast should start to froth, like this.

40 mins prep | 1 hr 20 mins rising and proofing, 25-35 mins baking | 2 small loaves

Ingredients:

- 1¼ cups warm water
- 1 tbsp sugar
- 1 x ¼oz (7g) packet active dry yeast
- 1 tsp salt
- 2¾ cups + 1 tbsp bread flour, plus extra for dusting
- 3 tbsp melted butter
- sunflower oil, for greasing
- 1 egg, beaten

Special equipment:

- 2 x 9 x 5in loaf pans, greased

1 Put ¼ cup of the warm (hand-hot) water in a small bowl with the sugar. Stir in the yeast and let stand for 10 minutes.

2 Stir the salt and flour together in a large bowl. Make a well in the center and pour in the melted butter and frothing yeast.

3 Rinse out the yeast bowl with 1 cup of the water and add to the flour. Mix to make a soft dough, adding more water as needed.

4 In the bowl, start forming the dough into a ball shape, ready to knead. Dust your work surface with flour to stop the dough from sticking.

5 Knead the dough for 10 minutes. Use the heel of your hand to push it away from you. Fold over the top end, turn it, and repeat.

6 Transfer the dough to a lightly greased bowl, cover it with plastic wrap, and leave in a warm place for 1 hour, to rise.

7 The dough is ready once it has doubled in size. It will look like this.

8 Punch down the dough— this means using your fists to squash out the air, then kneading it some more.

9 To make two small loaves, divide your dough into two equal-sized pieces.

10 Put each piece into a loaf pan. Cover the pans with greased plastic wrap and leave them to proof for about 20 minutes, or until doubled in size.

11 While the bread is proofing, preheat your oven to 400°F (200°C). Brush the loaves with beaten egg.

12 Bake them for 25–35 minutes, until they are golden on top and hollow-sounding when tapped underneath.

Baguette

This long, thin bread is sometimes called a French stick. To bake it, you first need to make a "sponge," which is a starter dough that rises for 12 hours. Then you add the sponge to the other ingredients to make a delicious bread.

30 mins prep | 12 hrs or overnight fermenting, 3½ hrs rising and proofing, 20 mins baking | 2 loaves

Ingredients:

For the sponge:

- ⅛ tsp active dry yeast
- ¼ cup white or whole wheat bread flour
- 1 tbsp rye flour
- Vegetable oil, for greasing

For the dough:

- 1 tsp active dry yeast
- 1¾ cups + 2 tbsp white or whole wheat bread flour, plus extra for dusting
- ½ tsp salt

Traditional baguettes are made from white flour. They are lighter than ones made from whole wheat flour.

16

1 Place the whole wheat or white flour in a large bowl with the rye flour. Dissolve the yeast in ¼ cup of lukewarm water. Add to the bowl.

2 Form a sticky, loose dough and place in a greased bowl, with room for it to expand.

3 Cover with plastic wrap and put in a cool place to rise for at least 12 hours.

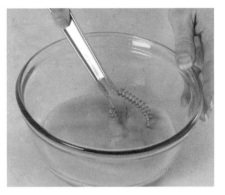

4 To make the dough, dissolve the yeast in ⅓ cup lukewarm water, whisking continuously.

5 Put the risen sponge, flour, and salt into a large bowl and pour in the yeast liquid.

6 Stir it all together with a wooden spoon to form a soft dough.

Continue

Continued

Baguettes were first baked in the 18th century in France.

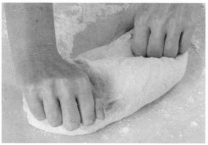

7 Knead for 10 minutes on a floured surface until smooth, glossy, and elastic.

8 Put in a greased bowl, cover with plastic wrap, and leave to rise in a warm place for 2 hours.

9 Put it on a floured surface. Punch it down. Carefully divide into 2 equal portions.

10 Knead briefly and shape each piece into a rectangle. Tuck one short edge into the center.

11 Press down firmly, fold over the other short edge, and press firmly again.

12 Shape the dough into a rounded oblong. Pinch to seal and turn seam-side down.

13 Shape into a long, thin log shape that is 1½in (4cm) wide.

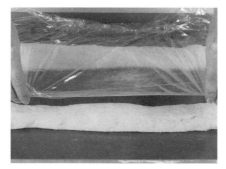

14 Place the loaves on a baking sheet and cover with greased plastic wrap and a clean dish towel.

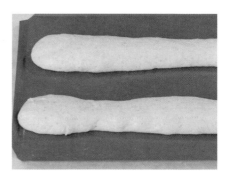

15 Keep in a warm place for 1½ hours, until doubled in size. Preheat the oven to 425°F (220°C).

You can put the baguettes back in the oven to freshen on the day after they are baked.

The crusty bit at the end of the baguette is called the "heel."

16 Carefully slash each loaf deeply on the diagonal along the top.

17 Dust with a little flour, spray with water, and put the loaves in the oven.

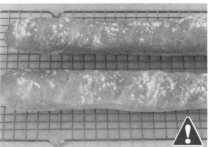

18 Bake for 20 minutes. Cool on a wire rack.

Sunflower pot loaves

Use terra-cotta plant pots to make these little loaves—perfect for sharing with your friends or family. Sunflower seeds are delicious and good for you, too.

45 mins prep, plus 5 hrs sealing pots | 2 hrs rising and proofing, 25–30 mins baking | 4 loaves

Follow step 1 to prepare the pots a day before making the loaves. Reseal the pots in the future.

Ingredients:

- 1½ cups + 1 tbsp bread flour, plus extra for dusting
- ¾ cup + 3 tbsp whole wheat flour
- 1 tsp salt
- 1 tsp granulated sugar
- 1 packet ½oz (7g) instant dry yeast
- 1 cup + 2 tbsp warm water
- 2 tbsp extra-virgin olive oil, plus extra for greasing
- ½ cup sunflower seeds
- a little milk, for brushing

Special equipment:

- four 5 x 4in (11 x 10cm) terra-cotta plant pots, scrubbed with hot soapy water, rinsed well, and dried thoroughly before starting

1 Preheat the oven to 400°F (200°C). Coat the pots with oil until no more oil is absorbed. Bake on oven sheets for 20 minutes. Turn the oven off. Leave to cool in the oven for 2 hours. Repeat the process.

2 Place the flour, salt, sugar, and yeast into a large bowl. Make a well in the center and pour in the water and olive oil. Mix to make a soft, but firm dough.

3 Turn the dough onto a lightly dusted work surface and knead well for at least 10 minutes.

4 Make a dip in the dough and add three-quarters of the sunflower seeds. Knead them into the dough.

5 Divide the dough into 4 balls. Place one in each pot. Cover the pots with a plastic bag. Leave until the dough has doubled in size.

6 Preheat the oven to 375°F (190°C). Brush milk on top of the loaves and sprinkle over the remaining seeds. Bake for 25–30 minutes, or until golden.

Turn out the bread and enjoy!

How flour is made

Flour is made by grinding wheat grains to make a fine powder. This is done in a factory called a mill. Here's what the process looks like, from field to final flour.

1 FARMED

Wheat is grown in large fields. A combine harvester cuts wheat down and separates the grains from the stalks.

Come and see the mill!

2 DELIVERED

Trucks collect the wheat from the farm and deliver it to the mill. Some mills try to use wheat grown nearby; others use wheat from all over the world.

Wheat delivery!

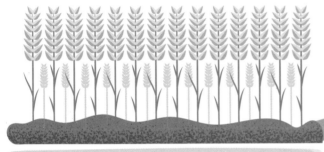

Wheat takes about four months to grow if it is planted in the spring, or eight months if it is planted in autumn.

5 SPLIT

The wheat is split open using steel rollers with tiny "teeth." The two rollers move at different speeds.

6 ROLLED

The split wheat then travels through many more sets of rollers.

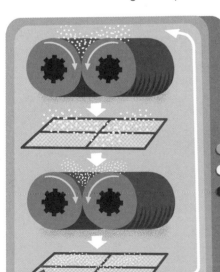

The split grain must be ground further before it becomes flour.

The grains of wheat are cracked open between the spinning rollers.

The flour gets smoother and finer as it travels through the rollers.

7 SIEVED

The flour then goes through a sifter, which sieves it, taking out any big pieces of the wheat grain.

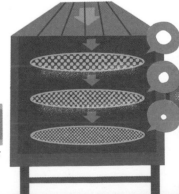

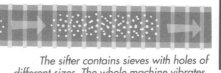

The sifter contains sieves with holes of different sizes. The whole machine vibrates, shaking the flour down through it.

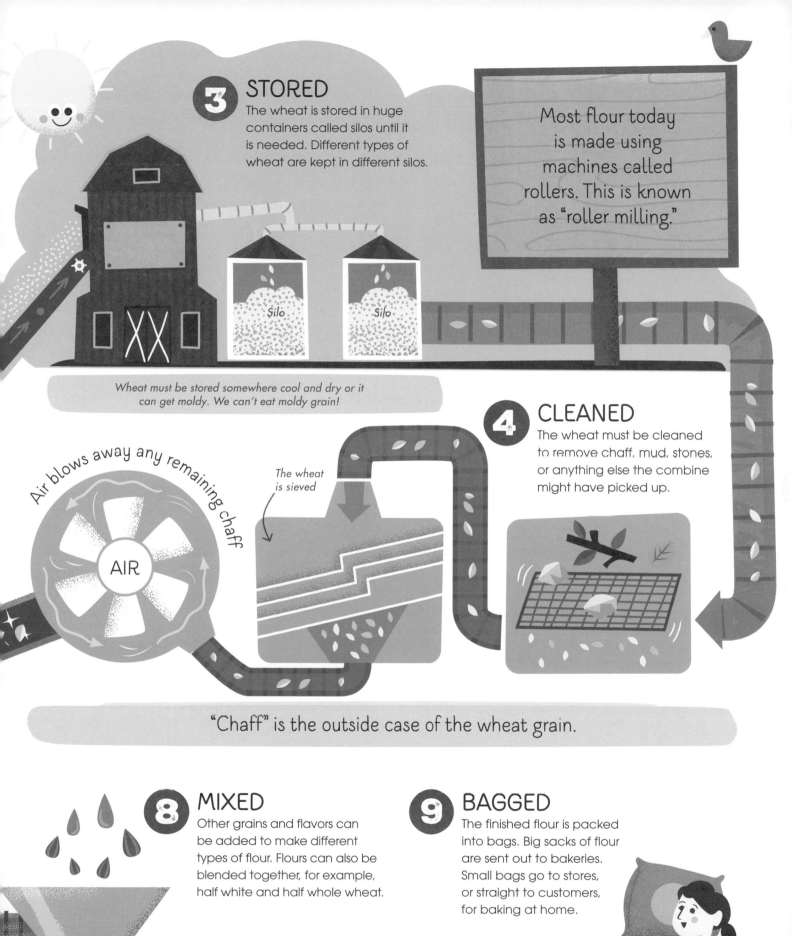

3 STORED

The wheat is stored in huge containers called silos until it is needed. Different types of wheat are kept in different silos.

Most flour today is made using machines called rollers. This is known as "roller milling."

Silo

Silo

Wheat must be stored somewhere cool and dry or it can get moldy. We can't eat moldy grain!

Air blows away any remaining chaff

The wheat is sieved

AIR

4 CLEANED

The wheat must be cleaned to remove chaff, mud, stones, or anything else the combine might have picked up.

"Chaff" is the outside case of the wheat grain.

8 MIXED

Other grains and flavors can be added to make different types of flour. Flours can also be blended together, for example, half white and half whole wheat.

9 BAGGED

The finished flour is packed into bags. Big sacks of flour are sent out to bakeries. Small bags go to stores, or straight to customers, for baking at home.

23

Bagels

These soft, springy bagels are perfect for breakfast or lunchtime—slice them open and spread with butter, or sandwich them together with a filling of your choice.

40 mins prep

3 hrs rising and proofing, 20–25 mins baking

Serves 8–10

Ingredients:

- 3¼ cups bread flour, plus extra for dusting
- 2 tsp fine salt
- 2 tsp granulated sugar
- 2 tsp active dry yeast
- 1 tbsp sunflower oil, plus extra for greasing
- 1 egg, beaten, for glazing

1 Put the flour, salt, and sugar in a bowl. In a separate bowl, mix the yeast with 1¼ cups lukewarm water.

2 Add the oil to the yeast, mix, then pour the liquid into the flour mixture, stirring it together to form a soft dough.

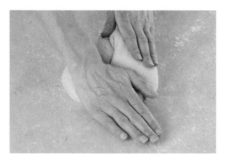

3 Knead on a floured surface for 10 minutes, until smooth. Put in a greased bowl. Cover with plastic wrap and leave in a warm place for 1–2 hours, until doubled in size.

4 Put the dough on a floured surface, press it down to its original size, then divide into 8–10 pieces.

5 Take each piece of dough and roll it under your palm to make a fat log shape.

6 Using your palms, continue to roll it toward each end, until it is about 10in (25cm) long.

24

7 Take the dough and wrap it around your knuckles, so the join is on your palm.

8 Squeeze the ends gently together, then roll briefly to seal the join. The hole should still be big at this stage. Repeat to shape all the bagels.

9 Line two baking sheets with parchment paper and put the bagels on the sheets. Cover with plastic wrap and a dish towel. Leave in a warm place for up to 1 hour, until doubled in size.

Bagels are one of the only type of bread that is boiled before being baked.

10 Preheat the oven to 425°F (220°C). Carefully boil a large pan of water, then let it simmer. Cook the bagels in the water for 1 minute on each side.

11 Remove them from the water with a slotted spoon. Dry them briefly on a clean dish towel. Return the bagels to the baking sheets and brush them with the beaten egg.

12 Bake in the center of the oven for 20–25 minutes, until golden. Carefully remove from the oven and cool for at least 5 minutes on a wire rack before serving.

Pizza

You've very likely eaten pizza, but have you ever made your own? This pesto, sun-dried tomato, and mozzarella pizza is easy to make. Once you've mastered it, you can add different combinations of your favorite toppings.

20 mins prep

1 hr rising and proofing, 20–30 mins baking

4 pizzas

Ingredients:

- ½ tsp granulated sugar
- 1 tsp active dry yeast
- 1½ cups lukewarm water
- 3 cups bread flour, plus extra for dusting
- 1 tsp salt
- 1 tbsp olive oil

For the sauce:

- 1¼ cups tomato puree
- 2 tbsp tomato paste
- ½ tsp granulated sugar
- 1 tsp dried mixed herbs

For the topping:

- 8 tbsp pesto (2 tbsp for each pizza)
- 24 sun-dried tomatoes, chopped (6 for each pizza)
- 2 balls mozzarella, torn into small pieces (½ a ball for each pizza)
- extra virgin olive oil, for drizzling
- freshly ground black pepper

Special equipment:

- 2 x pizza pans

Olive oil

Pizza cutting wheel

Pesto and sun-dried tomatoes are a simple but delicious topping. Your pizza will be full of flavor!

Long ribbons of twirly zucchini make for a pretty pizza. This slice also features mushrooms.

1 Put the sugar, yeast, and water in a bowl; mix and leave for 5 minutes. In another bowl, sift the flour and salt. Then add the oil and the yeast mixture to the flour mixture.

2 Stir with a spoon to form a dough, then knead on a lightly floured surface for 5 minutes. Place in a bowl, cover with a clean damp cloth, and leave in a warm place for 1 hour.

3 Meanwhile, make the tomato sauce. Place the sauce ingredients in a small pan and simmer gently for 5 minutes, then allow to cool.

4 Preheat the oven to 425°F (220°C). Using a floured hand, punch the dough to knock out the air, then knead lightly on a floured surface.

5 Divide the dough into four, then roll out each chunk into a circle that will fit the pizza pan. Place the dough for one pizza on the pan, followed by another circle for the other pan. Most ovens have two shelves, so you will need to bake the pizzas in two batches.

6 Spoon 3 tablespoons of the tomato sauce over each pizza crust. Then add dollops of the pesto on top. Scatter with the sun-dried tomatoes and mozzarella. Add a drizzle of olive oil and a sprinkling pepper. Bake for 10–15 minutes, or until the cheese is golden. Carefully cut the pizza into slices.

This is called "pizza bianca"—it has garlic, spinach, and ricotta cheese, with no tomato sauce.

Bread flour

This is a white flour made from wheat that contains lots of a type of protein called gluten. Bread flour is made from the inside of the wheat grain, which is called the endosperm. It uses about 75 percent of the wheat grain.

Malted grain flour

This is bread flour with malted grains added to it. Malting is when cereal grains are made to germinate, or begin growing, by being soaked in water. They then have hot air blown over them to make them dry out. The malted grains are soft and tasty.

Added ingredients

All sorts of things can be blended into flours to make different flavors. For example, **herbs, sun-dried tomatoes, onion, and honey.**

Seeded flour

This white flour with seeds mixed in is used to make delicious seeded breads. Flours may include just one type of seed or a mixture, including sesame, poppy, and sunflower.

Baking powder

Self-rising flour

This is all-purpose flour mixed with baking powder. It is mainly used for baking cakes.

Brown flour

This is partway between bread flour and whole wheat flour, with about 85 percent of the wheat grain used.

All-purpose

A wheat flour, usually used for making cakes, cookies, and pastry, it is made from softer wheat than bread flour.

Flour

Flour is a powder made by grinding up the edible seeds (grains) of types of grasses called cereals. **Most flour is made from a cereal called wheat.**

Spelt flour

This is made from an ancient grain called spelt. It is often used for baking sourdough bread.

Whole wheat

This is wheat flour milled from the whole wheat grain—none of the rougher parts, such as bran or germ, are removed. It makes a heavy loaf with a nuttier flavor than white flour.

Gluten-free flour

Wheat contains a protein called gluten, which some people are unable to eat. Here are some examples of flours made from things that don't contain gluten.

Gluten-free bread flour

Usually, this is made from a mixture of different flours. To make gluten-free bread, you need to follow a special recipe—you can't use gluten-free flour with a wheat bread recipe.

Gram flour

This flour is made from chickpeas. It is often used in traditional Indian cooking.

Buckwheat flour

Buckwheat may have "wheat" in its name, but it's actually a herb related to rhubarb. It has grainlike seeds that have been used to make flour for hundreds of years.

Rice flour

Rice isn't just eaten as whole grains! Flour made from ground-up rice can be used to bake cakes and bread.

Gluten—free bread

Gluten-free bread uses a special ingredient called xanthan gum to trap the air bubbles in the dough. You can buy preblended gluten-free bread flour or make a mixture yourself—two mixes are suggested here.

20 mins prep | 1 hr rising, 35 mins baking | 1 loaf

Ingredients:

- 2¾ cups gluten-free white or brown bread flour blend (see panel), plus extra for dusting
- 2 tsp instant dry yeast
- 1 tsp salt
- 1 tbsp granulated sugar
- 1¼ cups warm water
- 2 eggs, 1 beaten, for brushing
- 2 tbsp vegetable oil, plus extra for greasing
- 1 tsp vinegar

Special equipment:

- 9 x 5in bread pan, lightly greased

Rice flour is often used in gluten-free bread.

Rice plant

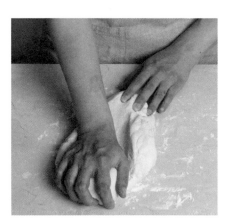

White gluten—free flour mix:

Makes 4¼ cups
- 2¾ cups white rice flour
- ¾ cup potato starch
- ½ cup tapioca starch
- ¼ cup cornstarch
- 4 tsp xanthan gum

Brown gluten—free flour mix:

Makes 4¼ cups
- 2¾ cups brown rice flour
- ¾ cup potato starch
- ½ cup tapioca starch
- ¼ cup cornstarch
- 4 tsp xanthan gum

1 Sift the flour, yeast, and salt into a large bowl, then stir in the sugar. Measure 1¼ cups lukewarm water into a liquid measuring cup, add the egg, oil, and vinegar and whisk with a fork.

2 Make a well in the center of the dry ingredients. Pour in the wet ingredients and mix well. Bring the mixture together with your hands to form a dough.

3 Turn the dough onto a lightly floured surface and knead for about 5 minutes, or until smooth.

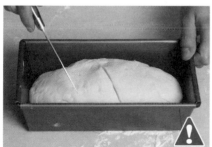

4 Shape the dough into a rectangle roughly the size of the pan and place it inside the pan. Carefully make 3 slashes on the top with a sharp knife. Cover with plastic wrap. Leave in a warm place to rise for 1 hour.

5 Preheat the oven to 425°F (220°C). Brush the top of the loaf with egg—this will help to color it. Then sprinkle it with a little flour.

6 Bake for 35 minutes, or until the loaf is risen and golden brown on top. Carefully remove from the pan, transfer to a baking sheet, and bake for another 10 minutes. Remove from the oven and let cool on a wire rack.

Rye bread

This crusty German loaf is chewy, with a stronger flavor than bread made from wheat flour alone.

40 mins prep

2 hrs 45 mins rising and proofing, 50–55 mins baking

1 loaf

Ingredients:

- 2½ tsp active dry yeast, dissolved in ¼ cup lukewarm water
- 1 tbsp dark molasses
- 1 tbsp caraway seeds
- 2 tsp salt
- 1 tbsp vegetable oil, plus extra for greasing
- 1 cup sparkling water
- 1⅓ cups rye flour
- 1 cup bread flour, plus extra for dusting
- polenta (fine yellow cornmeal), for dusting
- 1 egg white, beaten until frothy, for glazing

1 Put the dissolved yeast, molasses, two-thirds of the caraway seeds, salt, and oil into a bowl.

2 Pour the sparkling water into the bowl. Stir in the rye flour and mix together well with your hands.

3 Gradually add the bread flour until it forms a soft, slightly sticky dough.

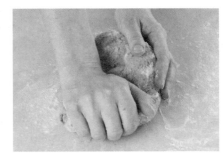

4 Knead for 8–10 minutes on a floured surface, until smooth and elastic, then put in an oiled bowl.

5 Cover with a damp dish towel. Put in a warm place for 1½–2 hours, until doubled in size.

6 Sprinkle a baking sheet with polenta. Punch down the dough on a floured work surface.

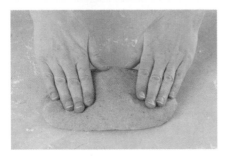

7 Cover with plastic wrap and let it rest for five minutes. Pat the dough into an oval, about 10in (25cm) long.

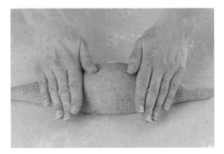

8 Roll it back and forth on the work surface, putting pressure on the ends to make them narrower.

9 Put on the baking sheet. Cover with plastic wrap and leave in a warm place for 45 minutes, until doubled in size.

10 Preheat the oven to 375°F (190°C). Brush the beaten egg white over the loaf to glaze.

11 Sprinkle with the remaining caraway seeds and press them into the dough.

12 Carefully make three diagonal slashes, about ¼in (5mm) deep, on top. Bake for 50–55 minutes. Put on a wire rack to cool.

Caraway seeds have a strong flavor similar to aniseed.

Ciabatta

This is an Italian bread, made with lots of olive oil. A good ciabatta should be well-risen and crusty, with large pockets of air in it.

Ciabatta is best eaten on the day it is baked.

30 mins prep

3 hrs rising and proofing, 30 mins baking

2 loaves

Ingredients:

- 2 tsp active dry yeast
- 2 tbsp olive oil, plus extra for greasing
- 2½ cups bread flour, plus extra for dusting
- 1 tsp sea salt

1 Dissolve the yeast in 1½ cups lukewarm water, then add the oil.

2 Put the flour and salt in a bowl. Make a well, pour in the yeast, and stir to form a soft dough.

3 Knead on a floured surface for 10 minutes, until the dough is smooth and soft.

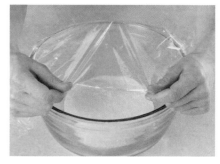

4 Put the dough in a lightly greased bowl and cover it loosely with plastic wrap.

5 Leave to rise in a warm place for 2 hours, until the dough has doubled in size. Turn onto a floured surface.

6 Gently punch down the dough, then divide it into 2 equal pieces.

Serve your ciabatta with olive oil for dipping.

7 Knead each piece briefly and shape each one into a long rectangle, around 12 x 4in (30 x 10cm).

8 Place each loaf on a lined baking sheet, with enough space to allow it to expand.

9 Cover loosely with plasstic wrap and a dish towel. Leave for 1 hour, until each loaf has doubled in size.

10 Preheat the oven to 450°F (230°C). Spray the loaves with a fine mist of water.

11 Bake for 30 minutes, removing from the oven carefully to spray the loaves with water every 10 minutes.

12 Remove from the oven when the top is golden. Allow to cool slightly, then tap the base—it should sound hollow.

Multigrain loaf

Adding seeds and grains to a loaf changes its texture, making it more interesting to eat. If you don't like sunflower seeds, you can try a different seed to add texture to the bread.

The more grains, the better the loaf!

45 mins prep   **3 hrs rising and proofing, 40–45 mins baking**   **2 loaves**

Ingredients:

- ½ cup + 3 tbsp sunflower seeds
- 5 tbsp rolled oats
- ⅓ cup wheat bran
- ½ cup polenta (fine yellow cornmeal), plus extra for the baking sheets
- 3 tbsp light brown sugar
- 1 tbsp salt
- 2½ tsp active dry yeast, dissolved in ¼ cup lukewarm water
- 1¾ cups lukewarm buttermilk
- 1½ cups whole wheat bread flour
- 1½ cups bread flour, plus extra for dusting
- 1 tbsp melted butter for greasing
- 1 egg white for glazing

Oat flakes

Sunflower seeds ↗

1 Preheat the oven to 350°F (180°C). Cook the seeds on a sheet in the oven for 5–7 minutes, until browned. Carefully remove from the oven, allow to cool, then coarsely chop.

2 Put the sunflower seeds, rolled oats, wheat bran, polenta, brown sugar, and salt in a large bowl. Add the dissolved yeast and buttermilk, and mix with your hands.

3 Stir in the whole wheat flour and half of the bread flour and mix well with your hands. Add the remaining bread flour; the dough should be soft and slightly sticky.

4 Knead the dough on a well floured surface for 8–10 minutes, until it is smooth and elastic. If the dough sticks while kneading, flour the work surface again.

5 Grease a large bowl with the butter. Put the dough in the bowl and flip it to butter the surface. Cover the bowl with a damp dish towel. Let the dough rise in a warm place for 1½–2 hours, until doubled in size.

6 Sprinkle two baking sheets with polenta. Put the dough on a lightly floured work surface and punch it down.

7 Cut the dough in half. With floured hands, pat one piece of dough into a rough 8 x 2in (20 x 5cm) rectangle, leaving the corners rounded. Put it on one of the baking sheets, and repeat to shape the remaining dough.

8 Cover with a dry dish towel, and leave to rise in a warm place for about 1 hour, until doubled in size. Preheat the oven to 375°F (190°C). Beat the egg white until just frothy. Brush the loaves with the egg white.

9 Bake for 40–45 minutes, until well browned. Carefully remove from the oven. Hold a loaf in a dish towel and tap the bottom with your knuckles; the bread should sound hollow. Move to a wire rack to cool completely.

Let your bread completely cool before carefully slicing it up.

Pita

Pita bread is from the Middle East. It puffs up as it cooks, making a big air pocket in the middle.

Bagels

First baked in Poland, these ring-shaped rolls are now popular everywhere, and particularly in the US.

Pita breads are flat and oval-shaped.

Bread

There are thousands of different types of bread. Almost every culture in the world has at least one type of its own. Here are just a few well-known examples.

Pistolets

These little rolls are from Belgium. They are crispy on the outside and soft in the middle.

The word "ciabatta" means "slipper bread."

Bao

These soft, steamed buns were originally from China, but are now eaten all over the world.

Ciabatta

An Italian bread made with olive oil, it was invented in 1982, as an Italian response to the very popular French baguette.

These pockets are for adding fillings.

Cottage loaf

This traditional loaf has two parts—a small round loaf on top of a larger round loaf.

Suikerbrood

This Dutch bread has big pieces of sugar mixed into its dough, and even more sugar dusted across the top.

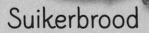

Marraqueta

This soft Chilean bread is split into four parts. It is easy to rip it apart with your hands.

Rieska

This Finnish flatbread is made with barley or rye flour. Sometimes it also contains potato.

Soda bread

With baking powder as a rising agent, this bread is very quick to make. It is popular in Ireland.

Arepas

These flatbreads made from cornmeal are popular in Venezuela, Colombia, and Panama.

Pretzels

Pretzel dough is stretched out and then shaped into knots. Pretzels were originally from Germany.

Cake bread

Brioche has so many delicious extra ingredients in its dough that it can be thought of as a cross between bread and cake. It is often eaten as a breakfast treat.

Khobz

This round flatbread is eaten with most meals in Morocco. It's perfect for scooping up other food.

This pattern is made by cutting the baguette before it is baked.

Brioche

Brioche dough contains lots of butter and eggs, making it soft and rich. It was first made in France.

Baguette

This French bread is long and thin, with a crisp crust.

Naan

This Indian bread is sometimes made with yeast and sometimes without. It is cooked in a circular oven called a tandoor.

Challah

This braided bread is enriched with eggs and decorated with sesame seeds. It is eaten to celebrate the Jewish sabbath, Shabbat.

Cornbread

This tasty, sweet-corn-filled bread is traditional in the Southern US. It is super quick to make and goes well with soups and stews.

20 mins prep   20–25 mins baking   Serves 8

Ingredients:

- 4 tbsp unsalted butter, melted and cooled, plus extra for greasing
- 2 fresh corncobs, about 7oz (200g) weight of kernels
- 1 cup fine yellow cornmeal or polenta
- ¾ cup bread flour
- ¼ cup granulated sugar
- 1 tbsp baking powder
- 1 tsp salt
- 2 eggs
- 1 cup milk

Special equipment:

- 9in (23cm) oven-safe, cast-iron frying pan or similar-sized, loose-bottomed round cake pan

1 Preheat the oven to 425°F (220°C). Grease the pan with butter. Place in the oven.

2 Carefully cut away the kernels from the cobs and scrape off any pulp from the cob with the back of the knife.

3 Sift the polenta, flour, sugar, baking powder, and salt into a bowl. Add the corn.

4 In a small bowl, whisk together the eggs, melted butter, and milk.

5 Pour three-quarters of the milk mixture into the flour mixture and stir.

6 Continue mixing in the dry ingredients, adding the remaining milk mixture. Stir until smooth.

↰ Sweet corn

7 Carefully take the hot pan out of the oven and pour in the batter—it should sizzle.

8 Quickly brush the top with melted butter. Bake for 20–25 minutes.

9 When the bread is fully baked, a skewer will come out clean. Cool slightly on a wire rack before serving.

Serve your cornbread warm.

Pretzels

First made in Germany, these breads are now popular all over the world. They are surprisingly easy and fun to make—read on to learn how to shape the perfect pretzel.

50 mins prep

1½–2½ hrs rising and proofing, 20 mins baking

Serves 16

Ingredients:

- 2¾ cups bread flour, plus extra for dusting
- 1 cup all-purpose flour
- 1 tsp salt
- 2 tbsp granulated sugar
- 2 tsp active dry yeast
- 1 tbsp sunflower oil, plus extra for greasing

For the glaze:

- ¼ tsp baking soda
- coarse sea salt, or 2 tbsp sesame seeds
- 1 egg, beaten, for glazing

Pretzels are a symbol of good luck.

Quick-working pretzel bakers can loop 40 pretzels in one minute!

1 Put the two types of flour, salt, and sugar into a large bowl.

2 Sprinkle the yeast over 1¼ cups lukewarm water. Stir, leave for 5 minutes, then add the oil.

3 Gradually pour the liquid into the flour mixture, stirring to form a soft dough.

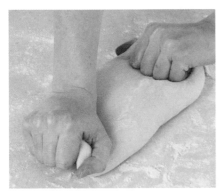

4 Knead for 10 minutes, until smooth and soft. Transfer to a greased bowl.

5 Cover loosely with plastic wrap and leave in a warm place for 1–2 hours, until nearly doubled in size.

6 Turn the dough onto a lightly floured work surface and gently punch it down.

Continue →

Continued →

A perfect ↗
pretzel

7 With a sharp knife, carefully cut the dough neatly into 16 equal pieces.

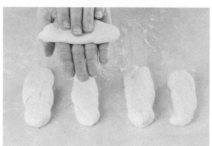

8 Take each piece of dough and roll it between your palms to make a log shape.

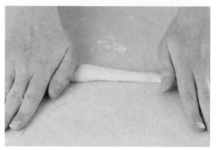

9 Using your palms, continue to roll the dough toward each end, until it is 18in (45cm) long.

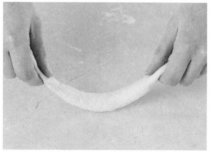

10 If difficult to stretch, hold by either end and rotate in a looping action, like a jump rope.

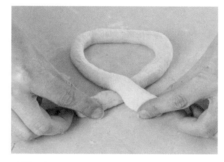

11 Take each end of the dough and cross each end over the other, forming a circle.

12 Now twist the ends around each other as though they had linked arms.

13 Secure the ends to the sides of the pretzel; it will appear fairly loose at this stage.

14 Repeat to make 16 pretzels. Put them on baking sheets lined with parchment paper.

15 Cover with plastic wrap and a dish towel. Leave in a warm place for 30 minutes, until puffed up.

Look, I'm beautiful!

16 Preheat the oven to 400°F (200°C). Mix the baking soda with 2 tablespoons of boiling water.

17 Brush the pretzels with the mixture. This gives them a dark color and makes them chewy on the outside.

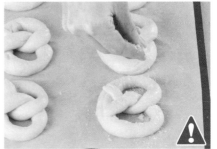

18 Scatter flakes of sea salt or sesame seeds over the brushed pretzels. Bake for 15 minutes.

19 Remove from the oven and brush with a little beaten egg. Bake for another 5 minutes.

20 Remove from the oven. The pretzels should be dark golden brown with a shiny finish.

21 Transfer to a wire rack and leave to cool for at least 5 minutes before serving.

Inside a bakery

Baking bread to sell in stores is a little different than baking at home. Most bakers use at least a few machines so they can make lots of bread more quickly and easily than they could by hand.

① DELIVERY

Flour is delivered to the bakery. Bakers get through a lot of flour in a week! Most will need weekly deliveries.

Flour

Flour sacks

The flour is piled up in tall stacks.

To make 1,000 loaves of bread, a baker will need 32 sacks of flour, each weighing 35lb (16kg).

Bread being baked

⑦ BAKING

Now the sheets of bread are put into huge ovens to bake. Bakery ovens have lots of shelves so many loaves of bread can be baked at once.

⑥ SECOND PROOF

Once in their pans, the loaves are left to rise again.

The dough doubles in size.

⑧ COOLING

Once baked, the bread must cool before it is taken out of the pans.

The bread cools on big wire racks.

⑨ SLICING

Some bread is sliced up before it is sold. Special machines can slice a whole loaf in seconds.

Bread slicing machine

46

② MIXING

Most bakers don't mix or knead their dough by hand. The ingredients are poured into a huge mixing machine, which blends them together at high speed.

Water

Salt

This machine uses a big hook to mix the dough.

Flour

Yeast

③ BATCH PROOF

Once mixed up, the dough is left to proof. It rises slowly as the yeast gets to work.

The dough gets bigger as it rises.

Dough

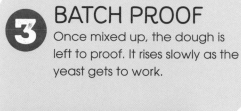

⑤ SHAPING

The loaves are shaped and put into the pans they will be baked in.

Loaf pan

④ SPLITTING

After proofing, the dough is divided into loaf-sized portions. Bigger bakeries might use a dividing machine to do this.

Dough dividing machine

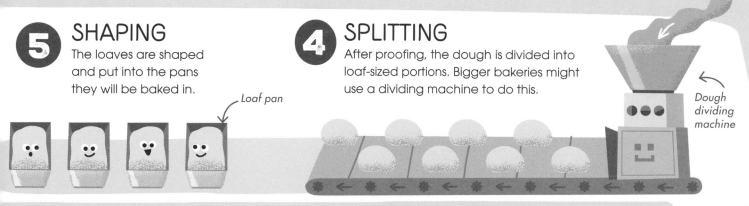

Loaves of bread can be made in pans or put right onto a baking sheet.

⑩ FOR SALE

Finally, the bread is ready to be sold. It is freshly made and delicious!

Bakery

To have bread ready to sell when the bakery opens, bakers start work very early in the morning, at 4 a.m. or even earlier!

Focaccia

Focaccia is an Italian flatbread pitted with fingertip-sized dimples. It is often flavored with herbs, cheese, tomatoes, or olives.

20 mins prep   2 hrs rising, 20–25 mins baking   Serves 8

Ingredients:

- 5 tbsp olive oil—reserve 1 tbsp for dipping, plus extra for greasing
- 2 cups bread flour
- 2 tsp dry yeast
- 1 tsp salt
- sprigs of rosemary
- sea salt, for sprinkling

Special equipment:

- 11 x 7in (28 x 18cm) baking pan

Rosemary   Olive oil

1 Lightly grease the baking pan. Sift the flour into a large bowl and stir in the yeast and salt.

2 Make a well in the center and add 1 cup lukewarm water and the oil. Mix until it forms a smooth dough.

3 Knead on a clean surface for 10 minutes until smooth. Move to a clean bowl, cover with a dish towel, and leave to rise in a warm place for 1 hour.

4 Press the dough into the pan so it fills all the corners. Cover with plastic wrap. Leave to rise in a warm place for 1 hour.

5 Preheat the oven to 400°F (200°C). Use your fingertips to make dimples in the dough. Sprinkle salt and rosemary over the dough. Bake for 20–25 minutes, until golden and crispy.

Olive oil with balsamic vinegar

People have been baking foccacia for more than 2,000 years!

49

Easy sourdough loaf

This loaf is made with a special, living rising agent called a starter. The sourdough bread it creates is chewy and sour-tasting, with a firm, crunchy crust.

Look at my loaf!

40 mins prep | 3–5 days for starter, 7–11 hrs, plus overnight rising and proofing, 35–40 mins baking | 2 loaves

The starter needs to be made in advance.

For the starter:
- 1 tbsp active dry yeast
- 2 cups warm water
- 2 cups bread flour

For the sponge:
- 1⅔ cups bread flour, plus 3 tbsp to sprinkle
- 1 cup warm water

For the dough:
- 6⅓ cups bread flour, plus extra for sprinkling in the bowls
- 2 tsp salt
- 3½ tbsp honey
- vegetable oil, for greasing
- polenta (fine yellow cornmeal) for the baking sheets
- ice cubes

Special equipment:
- 2 x 8in (20cm) bowls

Making the starter:
Sourdough starter is a type of living yeast. Here's how to make a starter and then keep it alive.

1 Sprinkle the yeast over the flour in a bowl, then slowly add 2 cups warm water to make a smooth paste. Cover, and leave it in a warm place for 24 hours to ferment. It will become frothy, with a sour smell. Stir the starter, cover, and stir each day for 2–4 days.

2 After 2–4 days, drop a teaspoon of the mixture into warm water to test it. It will float in the water if it is ready. Throw the starter away if it's moldy or smells bad. Use the starter or refrigerate it until you're ready to do step 3.

TIP: Replenish the starter after use. If you use 1 cup of starter, then stir in 1 cup of flour and 1 cup of warm water. Refresh the starter weekly by taking out ½ cup of it and adding ¾ cup flour and ½ cup warm water.

Make the sponge:

3 Pour the starter into a large mixing bowl and stir in 1⅔ cups of bread flour and the cup of lukewarm water. Mix it thoroughly with your hands or a wooden spoon for 30–60 seconds. This mixture is called the sponge.

4 Sprinkle the sponge with 3 tablespoons of flour, cover the bowl with a damp dish towel, and put it in a warm place for 5–8 hours.

Make the dough:

5 Weigh 10oz (300g) of the sponge mixture into a large bowl and gradually stir in half the flour, salt, honey, and 1¾ cups of warm water. Then add the rest of the flour and mix well to make the dough. Discard any remaining sponge.

6 Turn the dough onto a floured work surface. Sprinkle it and your hands with flour and knead for 10 minutes, until it is smooth and elastic and forms a slightly wet ball. Add more flour to your work surface if you need to.

7 Brush a large bowl with oil. Put the dough in the bowl, then flip it, so it is lightly greased on both sides. Cover the bowl with a damp dish towel, then let the dough rise in a warm place for 2–3 hours, until doubled in size.

8 Line two 8in (20cm) bowls with cotton napkins and sprinkle with flour (or you can use bread proofing baskets). Turn the dough onto a lightly floured work surface and knead lightly, folding the dough a couple of times.

9 Cut your dough in half. Shape each piece into a loose ball. Put the balls upside down into the prepared bowls. Cover them with dry dish towels and place the bowls in the fridge overnight. Take out of the fridge to reach room temperature.

10 Preheat the oven to 450°F (230°C). Set a roasting pan to heat in the oven on a lower rack. Sprinkle two baking sheets with polenta. Turn the loaves onto the prepared baking sheets. With a sharp knife, carefully cut three slashes, ½in (1cm) deep, into the top of each loaf, then add three more, making a crisscross pattern.

11 Put the loaves into the heated oven and carefully drop ice cubes into the hot roasting pan, to create steam in your oven. Bake the loaves for 20 minutes, then reduce the heat to 400°F (200°C) and bake for another 15–20 minutes, until well browned. Let the loaves cool on a wire rack.

Brioche des rois

This bread's name means the "brioche of kings" in French.
It is traditionally eaten at Epiphany, on January 6, when
the Three Kings are said to have arrived in Bethlehem.

25 mins prep

6 hrs rising and proofing, 25–30 mins baking

Serves 10-12

Ingredients:

- 2½ tsp active dry yeast
- 2 tbsp granulated sugar
- 5 eggs, beaten
- 3 cups bread flour, plus extra for dusting
- 1½ tsp salt
- vegetable oil, for greasing
- 12 tbsp unsalted butter, cubed and softened

For the filling and glaze:

- 1 egg, lightly beaten
- 1¾oz (50g) mixed candied fruit (orange and lemon zest, candied cherries, and angelica), chopped
- 2 tbsp coarse sugar crystals (optional)

Special equipment:

- 10in (25cm) ring mold (optional)
- ramekin

Angelica

Candied fruit

1 Whisk the yeast, sugar, and 2 tablespoons lukewarm water. Leave for 10 minutes, then mix in the eggs.

2 In a large bowl, sift together the flour and salt.

3 Make a well in the flour and pour in the eggs and yeast mixture.

4 Use a fork and then your hands to bring everything together and form a sticky dough. Turn the dough onto a lightly floured work surface.

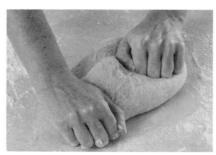

5 Knead the dough for 10 minutes, until elastic but still sticky. Put it in a greased bowl and cover with plastic wrap. Let rise in a warm place for 2–3 hours.

6 Transfer to a lightly floured surface and gently punch down the dough.

7 Put one-third of the butter on the dough. Fold the dough over the butter and knead gently for 5 minutes. Repeat until all the butter is used up. Keep kneading until no streaks of butter show.

8 Form the dough into a round and work it into a ring. Lightly grease a baking sheet and transfer the ring to the sheet or ring mold (if using).

9 Use a ramekin to keep the shape of the hole. Cover with plastic wrap and a dish towel. Leave to proof for 2–3 hours in a warm place, until doubled in size. Preheat the oven to 400°F (200°C).

This is a bread fit for kings! Please join me in my royal feast.

The candied fruit sparkles on top of the baked brioche.

10 Brush the brioche with beaten egg. Sprinkle with candied fruit and sugar crystals (if using). Bake for 25–30 minutes, until golden brown. Leave to cool slightly, then carefully turn onto a wire rack.

Tortoise bread rolls

These rolls are easy to make and fun to shape. You can eat them as they are or make them into a sandwich by adding a tasty filling.

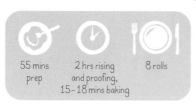

55 mins prep

2 hrs rising and proofing, 15–18 mins baking

8 rolls

Ingredients:

- ⅓ cup milk, plus extra, if needed
- 4 tbsp unsalted butter, cubed, plus extra for greasing
- 2 tbsp granulated sugar
- 3 tsp active dry yeast
- 2 eggs, plus 1 yolk, for glazing
- 2 tsp salt
- 3½ cups bread flour, plus extra for dusting
- small writing icing tube, for decoration
- raisins, for decoration

The icing will help you attach the eyes!

1 Bring the milk to a boil. Put ¼ cup into a small bowl and let it cool to lukewarm. Add the butter and sugar to the remaining milk in the pan and stir until melted. Cool to lukewarm.

2 Sprinkle the yeast over ¼ cup of milk. Leave for 5 minutes to dissolve. Stir once. In a large bowl, lightly beat the eggs. Add the sweetened milk, salt, and dissolved yeast.

3 Gradually stir in the flour until the dough forms a ball. It should be soft and slightly sticky. If it's too dry, then slowly add up to 3 tablespoons of extra milk.

4 Knead the dough on a floured work surface for 5–7 minutes, until smooth. Put in a greased bowl. Cover with plastic wrap. Put in a warm place for 1–1½ hours, until doubled in size.

5 Line two baking sheets with parchment paper. Punch down the dough, then place it on a floured work surface.

6 Carefully cut the dough in half, using a table knife.

7 Carefully cut one-half of the dough into 8 equal chunks. These will be the tortoise body shapes.

8 Roll each chunk into a round ball shape, then place the balls on the lined baking sheets.

9 Cut the remaining dough into three. Use two of the pieces to make 8 balls for the heads. Then roll 32 smaller balls for the feet. Use water to stick your tortoises together.

10 Cover the tortoises with a dish towel. Leave in a warm place for 30 minutes. Score a cross on each roll carefully.

11 Preheat the oven to 425°F (220°C). Beat the egg yolk with a tablespoon of water. Brush the rolls with the egg.

12 Bake for 15–18 minutes, or until golden brown. Carefully remove from the oven and cool on a wire rack. Use a dab of icing to attach the raisin eyes.

Cinnamon rolls

This dough is enriched with butter. It makes soft, sweet rolls packed with flavor. To bake them for breakfast, leave them to proof overnight in the fridge after step 11.

40 mins prep
4 hrs rising and proofing, 25–30 mins baking
Serves 10–12

Ingredients:

- ½ cup water
- ½ cup milk
- 7 tbsp unsalted butter, plus extra for greasing the pan
- 2 tsp active dry yeast
- ¼ cup granulated sugar
- 3 cups all-purpose flour, sifted, plus extra for dusting
- 1 tsp salt
- 1 egg, plus 2 egg yolks
- vegetable oil, for greasing the bowl

For the filling and glaze:

- 3 tbsp ground cinnamon
- ⅔ cup light brown sugar
- 2 tbsp unsalted butter, melted
- 1 egg, lightly beaten
- ¼ cup granulated sugar

Special equipment:

- 12in (30cm) round springform cake pan

1 In a pan, heat the water, milk, and butter until just melted. Let it cool to just warm. Whisk in the yeast and a tablespoon of the sugar. Cover for 10 minutes.

2 Put the flour, salt, and remaining sugar in a large bowl. Make a well in the center and pour in the warm milk mixture.

3 In a small bowl, whisk the egg and yolks, then add to the mixture. Combine to form a coarse dough.

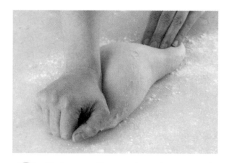

4 Put on a floured surface and knead for 10 minutes. Add extra flour if it is too sticky.

5 Grease a bowl with the oil. Place the dough in the bowl and cover with plastic wrap and keep in a warm place for 2 hours, until well risen.

6 Prepare the filling by mixing 2 tablespoons of the cinnamon with the brown sugar.

7 When the dough has risen, turn it onto a floured work surface and gently punch it down. Roll it into a rectangle about 16 x 12in (40 x 30cm).

8 Brush with the melted butter and scatter the filling on top. Leave a ½in (1cm) border on one side and brush it with the egg. Press the filling with your hand to stick it to the dough.

9 Roll the dough up, working toward the border. Do not roll too tightly.

10 Carefully cut into 10–12 equal pieces using a serrated knife, taking care not to squash the rolls. Grease and line the pan.

11 Pack in the rolls, cover with plastic wrap, and proof for 1–2 hours, until well risen. Preheat the oven to 350°F (180°C).

12 Brush with egg and carefully bake for 25–30 minutes. Heat 3 tablespoons of water and 2 tablespoons of sugar until dissolved. Carefully brush on the rolls. Sprinkle a mix of the remaining sugar and cinnamon on top, then turn onto a wire rack to cool.

A tasty breakfast treat!

Soda bread

This is one of the quickest and easiest breads to make. It has a light, cakelike texture and the dough doesn't need to be kneaded.

15 mins prep	35–40 mins baking	1 loaf

Ingredients:

- butter, for greasing
- 4 cups whole wheat flour, plus extra for dusting
- 1½ tsp baking soda
- 1½ tsp salt
- 2 cups buttermilk, plus extra, if needed

Buttermilk

Baking soda

1 Preheat the oven to 400°F (200°C). Grease a baking sheet with butter.

2 Sift the flour, baking soda, and salt into a large bowl, adding in any leftover bran.

3 Mix thoroughly to combine and make a well in the middle of the dry ingredients.

4 Slowly pour the buttermilk into the center of the well.

5 With your hands, quickly draw in the flour to make a soft, slightly sticky dough.

6 Do not overwork the dough. Add a little more buttermilk if it seems dry.

The four quarters of the soda bread are called "farls."

7 Turn the dough onto a floured surface and quickly shape into a round loaf.

8 Put the loaf on the baking sheet and pat it down into a round, about 2in (5cm) high.

9 Carefully make a cross ½in (1cm) deep in the top of the loaf with a sharp knife.

10 Bake the loaf for 35–40 minutes, until brown. Carefully remove from the oven.

11 When cooked and cooled slightly, turn the loaf over and tap the bottom. The bread should sound hollow.

12 Put the bread on a wire rack and allow to cool completely before serving.

Bread in numbers

People have made and eaten bread for thousands of years. Here are a few final facts for you about farming, milling, baking, and bread-eating.

Wheat farming began around 10,000 years ago.

CHINA PRODUCES MORE WHEAT THAN ANY OTHER COUNTRY IN THE WORLD.

IN FRANCE, IT IS THOUGHT TO BE BAD LUCK TO PUT A LOAF OF BREAD UPSIDE DOWN.

While digging in the remains of the ancient Roman city of Herculaneum, scientists found a 2,000-year-old loaf of bread still inside an oven. The recipe was then re-created by the British Museum.

Rúgbrauð is a type of Icelandic bread that is baked by being buried in a pot in the ground near a hot spring.

Bread is a symbol of

WELCOME

in Russia.

French bakeries are only allowed to call themselves bakeries if they make all their bread completely from scratch.

The first bread slicing machine was invented by Otto Frederick Rohwedder in Michigan in 1928. By 1933, 80 percent of the bread sold in the US was sliced and wrapped.

Boudin Bakery in San Francisco has been baking

SOURDOUGH

bread since 1849. They are still using their original sourdough starter.

The longest loaf of bread ever made was 3,975ft 0.69in (1,211.6m) lon

IT TAKES **9 SECONDS** FOR A COMBINE HARVESTER TO HARVEST ENOUGH WHEAT TO MAKE **70** LOAVES OF BREAD.

IT TAKES AROUND 350 EARS OF WHEAT TO MAKE ENOUGH FLOUR FOR A 28OZ (800G) LOAF OF BREAD.

One whole grain of wheat makes **20,000** particles of flour.

Americans eat an average of **53LB** (24K) of bread each every year.

Keeping your bread in the fridge is a bad idea—it becomes stale six times faster than it would at room temperature.

Before erasers were invented, the doughy part of a loaf of bread was used to get rid of unwanted pencil marks.

Germany has more types of bread than any other country in the world.

200

SANDWICHES ACCOUNT FOR **50** PERCENT OF THE BREAD EATEN IN THE UK.

It was made in Portugal and used 10,684lb (4,844kg) of flour.

Glossary

BATCH
The quantity of goods baked or made at one time. Baking in batches is usually done if you have limited space in the oven.

BEAT
Stirring or mixing quickly until smooth, using a whisk, spoon, or electric mixer.

CHAFF
The outside husk of the wheat grain.

COMBINE
Mixing ingredients together evenly.

DOUGH
The mixture of flour, water, salt, and yeast (and sometimes more ingredients) before it is baked into bread.

DRIZZLE
Pouring slowly, in a trickle.

ENDOSPERM
The inside part of the wheat grain.

FLOUR
A powder made by grinding up edible grains.

FOLD
Mixing ingredients together gently, to keep as much air in the mixture as possible.

GLAZE
Coating food in a liquid to give it a smooth, glossy surface.

GLUTEN
A type of protein present in wheat.

GRAIN
The seeds of the wheat plant.

GREASE
Rubbing butter or oil onto a baking sheet, pan, or tray to stop food from sticking to it.

KNEAD
Pressing and folding dough with your hands until it is smooth and stretchy. This distributes the yeast and helps the dough to rise.

LINE
Placing parchment paper or foil in a pan so that food won't stick to it.

LUKEWARM
Mildly warm.

MILL
A factory where wheat is ground into flour.

OVERWORK
If food is handled, beaten, or rolled out too many times then it doesn't work as well in a recipe.

PREHEAT
Turning the oven on and heating it to the correct temperature before baking food in it.

PROOF
The final rise of bread dough before baking.

PUNCH DOWN
Deflating risen dough with a gentle punch. This evens out the texture of the bread.

RISE
Dough gets bigger in size when left in a warm place.

SCORE
Making shallow cuts across the surface of the dough.

SIFT
Using a sieve to remove lumps from dry ingredients.

SIMMER
Cooking over low heat, so the liquid or food is bubbling gently but not boiling.

TEXTURE
The way something feels, e.g., soft, smooth, chunky, or moist.

TURN
Taking out of a pan or bowl and carefully laying on a surface.

WELL
A dip made in flour, in which to crack an egg or pour liquid.

YEAST
A type of fungus that when added to flour, water, and salt causes the mixture to rise.

Index

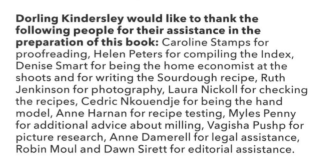

Senior Editor Carrie Love
Senior Art Editor Claire Patane
US Editor Margaret Parrish
US Senior Editor Shannon Beatty
Production Editor Abi Maxwell
Production Controller John Casey
Jacket Designer Claire Patane and Dheeraj Arora
Jacket Editor Carrie Love
Illustrator Diego Vaisberg
Additional designing Eleanor Bates,
Elaine Hewson, Polly Appleton, and Charlotte Bull
Managing Editor Penny Smith
Managing Art Editor Mabel Chan
Publishing Director Sarah Larter

First American Edition, 2021
Published in the United States by DK Publishing
1450 Broadway, Suite 801, New York, New York 10018

Text copyright © Elizabeth Davey 2021
Recipes, layout and design copyright © Dorling Kindersley Limited
DK, a Division of Penguin Random House LLC
21 22 23 24 25 10 9 8 7 6 5 4 3 2 1
001–323499–October/2021

ISBN: 978-0-7440-4212-2

DK books are available at special discounts when purchased in bulk for sales promotions, premiums, fund-raising, or educational use. For details, contact: DK Publishing Special Markets, 1450 Broadway, Suite 801, New York, New York 10018
SpecialSales@dk.com

The recipes contained in this book have been created for the ingredients and techniques indicated. The Publisher is not responsible for your specific health or allergy needs that may require supervision. Nor is the Publisher responsible for any adverse reactions you may have to the recipes contained in the book, whether you follow them as written or modify them to suit your personal dietary needs or tastes.

Printed and bound in China

For the curious
www.dk.com

Acknowledgments

Dorling Kindersley would like to thank the following people for their assistance in the preparation of this book: Caroline Stamps for proofreading, Helen Peters for compiling the Index, Denise Smart for being the home economist at the shoots and for writing the Sourdough recipe, Ruth Jenkinson for photography, Laura Nickoll for checking the recipes, Cedric Nkouendje for being the hand model, Anne Harnan for recipe testing, Myles Penny for additional advice about milling, Vagisha Pushp for picture research, Anne Damerell for legal assistance, Robin Moul and Dawn Sirett for editorial assistance.

**Material used in this book was previously published by DK:
Children's Cookbook (2004),
The Children's Baking Book (2010),
The Illustrated Step-by-Step Cook (2010),
Illustrated Step-by-Step Baking (2011),
Complete Children's Cookbook (2015),
The Gluten-free Cookbook (2015),
Cooking Step by Step (2018),
Bake It (2019),
The Vegetarian Cookbook (2019)**

Picture Credits
The publisher would like to thank the following for their kind permission to reproduce their photographs:

(Key: a-above; b-below/bottom; c-center; f-far; l-left; r-right; t-top)

5 Dorling Kindersley: Mattel INC (bl). 6 Getty Images / iStock: bergamont (fcrb). 7 Dorling Kindersley: Design Museum, London (cr). 8 123RF.com: Andrey Milkin (tr). Dreamstime.com: Dohnal (tl, clb); Stocksnapper (br). 9 Alamy Stock Photo: Blickwinkel / Laule (tr). Dreamstime.com: Natthawut Nungensanthia (br); Claudio Rampinini (bl). Getty Images / iStock: rvimages (tc). Shutterstock.com: PremiumVector (crb). 18 123RF.com: Andrey Milkin (tc). 29 Alamy Stock Photo: JG Photography (crb). Dreamstime.com: Mitgirl (tc). 30 Dreamstime.com: Anan Punyod (ca). 31 Dreamstime.com: Anan Punyod (tr). 32 Dreamstime.com: Dohnal (bl). 38 Dreamstime.com: Larisa Blinova (bl); Paul Brighton (cb); Food-micro (cla); Björn Wylezich (crb). Getty Images / iStock: bergamont (cra). 39 Alamy Stock Photo: Food / Peter Forsberg (tc). Getty Images / iStock: nehopelon (cra). Shutterstock.com: Kenyannature (cr)

Cover images: Front: 123RF.com: Andrey Milkin cla; Back: 123RF.com: Andrey Milkin bl

All other images © Dorling Kindersley
For further information see: www.dkimages.com